P9-CDI-581

At Issue

Location-Based Social Networking and Services

Other Books in the At Issue Series:

At Issue

Location-Based Social Networking and Services

Roman Espejo, Book Editor

GREENHAVEN PRESS
A part of Gale, Cengage Learning

GALE
CENGAGE Learning·

Farmington Hills, Mich • San Francisco • New York • Waterville, Maine
Meriden, Conn • Mason, Ohio • Chicago

Elizabeth Des Chenes, *Director, Content Strategy*
Douglas Dentino, *Manager, New Product*

For more information, contact:
Greenhaven Press
27500 Drake Rd.
Farmington Hills, MI 48331-3535
Or you can visit our Internet site at gale.cengage.com

For product information and technology assistance, contact us at

Gale Customer Support, 1-800-877-4253
For permission to use material from this text or product, submit all requests online at
www.cengage.com/permissions

Further permissions questions can be emailed to permissionrequest@cengage.com

Articles in Greenhaven Press anthologies are often edited for length to meet page requirements. In addition, original titles of these works are changed to clearly present the main thesis and to explicitly indicate the author's opinion. Every effort is made to ensure that Greenhaven Press accurately reflects the original intent of the authors. Every effort has been made to trace the owners of copyrighted material.

Cover image copyright © Images.com/Corbis.

LIBRARY OF CONGRESS CATALOGING-IN-PUBLICATION DATA

Location-based social networking and services / Roman Espejo, book editor.
    pages cm. -- (At issue)
  Includes bibliographical references and index.
  ISBN 978-0-7377-6842-8 (hardcover) -- ISBN 978-0-7377-6843-5 (pbk.)
  1. Online social networks. 2. Location-based services--Social aspects. 3. Privacy, Right of. I. Espejo, Roman, 1977-
  HM742.L63 2014
  006.7'54--dc23

                                                              2013048061

Printed in the United States of America
1 2 3 4 5 6 7 18 17 16 15 14

Contents

Introduction

In a 2012 report, the Pew Internet & American Life Project claims that one in twenty teens who have cell phones—or 6 percent—use location-based applications such as Foursquare or features found on social networks. "When focusing solely on cell phone users, fully 8 percent of teen cell users have used such a service on their cell phone to check in or share their location,"[1] states Amanda Lenhart, who directs the project's studies on children, teens, and families. According to the report, the use of location-based services jumps to 18 percent for teens who have smartphones. In addition, older teens use them much more than younger teens: 9 percent for fourteen- to seventeen-year-olds and less than 1 percent for twelve- to thirteen-year-olds. In fact, seventeen-year-olds led usage at 19 percent, more than triple that of fifteen- and sixteen-year-olds at 6 percent. The report concludes that other demographic factors do not appear to influence adolescents' use of such apps and features. "There are no statistically significant differences in use of location-based services by gender, race, household income, or parent's education level," Lenhart elaborates.

To some in the tech industry, location-based services are the next big thing in social networking for teens. In a 2011 report, youth marketing research firm Ypulse finds that 40 percent of students "checked in" at various locations and events, with high school students checking in more frequently at 45 percent. "It is a minority of young social media users who have done so, but the numbers are significant, particularly in comparison to the mere 4 percent of all adults who have

---

1. Amanda Lenhart, *Texting, Smartphones & Teens*, March 19, 2012. http://pewinternet .org/Reports/2012/ Teens-and-smartphones/What-teens-do-with-phones/Location -based-services.aspx.

checked in via social sites,"[2] asserts Melanie Shreffler, editor-in-chief of Ypulse. Other findings include that 67 percent of students check in at concerts, 64 percent at the movies, 63 percent at restaurants (non-fast food), and 52 percent at retailers. "A check-in at the sold-out concert, hot nightspot, or cool store ups their social street cred and shows others they're part of the latest trend," she observes. Furthermore, Ypulse maintains that adolescents are at ease with sharing where they are and what they're doing—even when marketers collect and analyze that data.

Nonetheless, others in the industry believe that the majority of youths are unaware of or disinterested in location-based services. Dubit, a British firm specializing in digital entertainment and media for children, purports in a 2011 survey that only 44 percent of British teens have heard of Facebook Places and 27 percent know about Foursquare. "Of the teens that are aware of the products, 5 percent use Foursquare, compared to 30 percent who use Places,"[3] Dubit insists. More than half of respondents indicate that they do not use the apps or features at all. "A significant 67 percent of the sample didn't use any of the services, with girls being less interested than boys with 76 percent not using any location application," the firm contends. The reasons cited by the respondents differ: 58 percent "didn't see the point," 45 percent view them as unsafe, 28 percent assume that their devices did not support the services, and 16 percent state that none of their friends use them. "Ultimately, teens just don't see the point of these offerings,"[4] argues Peter Robinson, who heads research at Dubit. Therefore, he advises that "brands who are using these platforms and the platform

---

2. As quoted in Michelle Atagana, "Location-Based Services: The New Social Currency for Teens," September 16, 2011. http://memeburn.com/2011/09/location-based-services-is-the-new-social-currency-for-teens.
3. "Location Services Failing to Grab Teen's Attention," Dubit, May 9, 2011. http://dubit.pressdoc.com/20511-location-services-failing-to-grab-teen-s-attention.
4. *Ibid.*

owners need to be telling teens why they should be using them and how they can do so safely."

Despite the conflicting research on location-based services and teens, the statistics seem to be encouraging for Foursquare, the preeminent location-based app in 2013. (Facebook Places and Gowalla, Foursquare's biggest rivals, were shut down in 2011 and 2012, respectively.) As of September 2013, it had forty million users globally, more than 4.5 billion check-ins with millions more daily, and 1.5 million businesses on its Merchant Platform. *At Issue: Location-Based Social Networking and Services* examines the growth and future of Foursquare and other geolocation technologies and addresses their implications on business, marketing, social interaction, and privacy. The varied analyses and divergent positions offered by experts, business leaders, and commentators highlight the possibilities and potential pitfalls of location-based services in an increasingly mobile world.

1

Be There or Be Square:
The Rise of Location-Based
Social Networking

Knowledge@Wharton

Knowledge@Wharton is the online business journal of the Wharton School at the University of Pennsylvania.

Young adults are flocking in droves to location-based social networks, particularly Foursquare. It is a smartphone app that enables users to "check-in" at various locations, letting their contacts know where they are and what they are doing—and vice versa. Due to its popularity, other social networking sites are adding location-based features to their sites. Apple's iPhone has driven the growth of location-based social networks as the first mobile device to have location-based features that are easy to use, mapping software, and developer-friendly app integration. Businesses jumping on Foursquare or similar sites to reach consumers are advised to use location-based social networking in their marketing strategies only if it is a good fit and provides a return on investment.

To find the hottest restaurant, bar or concert venue in town, many young adults are no longer checking in with their friends. They're "checking in" virtually via Foursquare, a location-based social networking site. Participants log onto the site and "check in" via smartphone to let contacts who are fellow users know where they are. At the same time, they learn what those users are doing—whether a co-worker is eating at the restaurant next door, or if friends are gathering at a night-club across town. As "check in" alerts are traded between phones, the people attached to them instantly become aware of the spots that are popular in their social circles.

Foursquare, which was founded by Dennis Crowley and Naveen Selvadurai, was introduced at the March 2009 South by Southwest music and interactive media festival in Austin, Texas. In recent weeks, the New York-based company has made headlines by gaining about 100,000 users in 10 days during this year's South by Southwest event. Web traffic to Four-square has increased by 400% since October 2009, according to the research firm Hitwise—and that doesn't even count us-ers who access the service via third party mobile applications.

The site currently has more than 800,000 members [30 million as of January 2013] "checking in" at locations around the globe. In addition to sharing their location with contacts, check-ins earn users points and digital merit badges through Foursquare's built-in game. For example, a "Bands on the Run" badge was offered to South by Southwest visitors who checked in at seven concerts in one day. The most coveted title is that of "mayor"—rewarded to the most frequent visitor to any given location.

While social networking sites—including Facebook, Yelp and Twitter—are taking notice of Foursquare's rising popular-ity and adding "check in" and location features to their sites, experts caution that function is more important than form. "Positioning a product as the new cool, hip thing is great for getting people to flood in, but it's also going to make people flood out quickly as people move onto the next hot thing," Wharton marketing professor Jonah Berger says. "For a prod-uct to persist, at some point it has to transition from a hip new thing to something that has functional value."

Although Foursquare and competitors like Gowalla [which shut down in March 2012] are the subject of most of the current headlines, experts say the true potential lies in companies knowing exactly where customers are and pitching offers or offering services based on the spots these customers frequent. As smartphones become more common and social networking gains a broader audience, consumers are consciously sharing more information than ever about their daily routines. That information makes it easier for businesses to advertise, or offer special discounts, that fit what someone is doing at a given moment. The challenge for Foursquare and other companies, observers suggest, is transitioning beyond buzz and finding uses for geo-targeting that are both profitable and practical.

The usage of phones that allow Internet access, and participation in social networking sites, grew significantly in recent years.

"Location is a broad variable that's going to be built into lots of different kinds of apps and services," says Kevin Werbach, a Wharton professor of legal studies and business ethics. "Social networking has obviously been a huge business phenomenon over the last few years. People have a virtual relationship with their friends but they also have a physical relationship in terms of where they are at any given time. Location is a valuable piece of information that can potentially enhance the richness of any kind of social interaction."

iPhone's Inflection Point

Location features were incorporated into mobile phones as early as 2000, but earlier social networking sites built around the technology, such as Dodgeball, failed to gain a foothold. Dodgeball, which had relied on text message blasts to update users on their friends' activities, had been founded by Crowley and then sold in 2005 to Google, which eventually shut it down.

"The inflection point for this was the iPhone," says Kevin Nakao, vice president of mobile and business search for web and mobile publisher WhitePages. "The iPhone was the first big device that got into the hands of a lot of consumers and added really easy-to-use location elements. They integrated mapping software into the device. Not only that, they made it easy for developers and publishers to integrate our applications." The iPhone has spawned such location-centric apps as a ski and snow report by outdoor gear retailer REI and a program called Flixster that allows users to search for movie times and reviews. Nakao notes that downloads of the White-Pages iPhone app increase significantly any time the program is featured on iTunes. In addition, he says, 80% of the campaigns offered via the application by major brands are geo-targeted, or displayed to consumers in specific markets that are chosen by the ad buyer.

The usage of phones that allow Internet access, and participation in social networking sites, grew significantly in recent years. In a 2009 survey by the Pew Research Center's Internet & American Life Project, 32% of adults reported using their mobile devices to surf the web, up from 24% in 2007. Only 8% of adults told Pew in 2005 that they had a profile on a social networking site; that number was 47% for all adults in 2009 and 72% for men and women ages 18–29. According to Hitwise, U.S. web traffic to location-based social networking sites has increased by 350% in the past year. Profiles of Foursquare users reflect the statistics; co-founder Selvadurai, 28, says most of those checking in on the site are college students or young professionals in their 20s and 30s who live in urban areas. The site initially launched only in large U.S. cities but since December [2009] has been available anywhere in the world. Tokyo, for example, is close to becoming second only to New York for having the largest number of user check-ins.

"Location has always been interesting, but now the technology has caught up," says Selvadurai. "We're finally in a position where you no longer have to go through carriers. There's no longer a lengthy process to get an app approved. Anyone can build [an application with a location feature]."

He and Crowley, 33, were interested in developing a networking site based on location because they thought the concept better lent itself to spontaneous meet-ups—the trading of tips and suggestions and other "serendipitous connections" that can be difficult when people live thousands of miles apart. They incorporated the game of points, badges and mayorships into Foursquare, thinking it would ignite users' competitive spirits and encourage them to explore their communities. "The idea of sharing is an honest one and one that is attractive no matter what kind of demographic you fit into. It's just a matter of teasing out the right rewards [for different age groups]," Selvadurai says. "We've actually heard stories of people using [Foursquare] to check into a playground with the intention of announcing to other parents that, 'Hey my kids are here. You should come and have a play date.'"

Foursquare has implemented a "cheater code" that employs phone GPS signals to verify that users are where they say they are.

Although Wharton operations and information management professor Kartik Hosanagar isn't surprised that young, urban-dwelling men and women are the early adopters, he believes location-based social networking has the potential to gain broader appeal because the services tap into a person's natural desire to belong to a community, and to gain social status by becoming a recognized "expert" in knowing the hotspots in his or her home turf. "Those are the types of things that go across generations. They're more fundamental," he says.

Marketing professor Eric Bradlow agrees, noting that "every product that penetrates the market starts with a segment. You don't mass market to start; you target a market and then expand to other segments." Location-based social networking sites, however, are already beginning to attract brands that appeal to a broader audience. A partnership between Foursquare and the Bravo television channel allows users to get tips and recommendations from the channel's personalities, and earn badges based on the channel's programs such as "Top Chef" or "Real Housewives of New York City." Austin, Texas-based Gowalla, which recently announced a similar partnership with the Travel Channel, worked with Chevrolet to offer a free ride promotion for visitors to South by Southwest.

Laura Wilson, a talent buyer for Philadelphia restaurant and concert venue World Café Live, was first exposed to Foursquare at South by Southwest. Anyone can add a location to Foursquare, and when Wilson signed on to add her business to the site, she found that hundreds of users had already been "checking in" there for months. Now World Café is planning to offer free food to each week's reigning "mayor." "It's something we need to pursue . . . because for us it's driving people in," she notes. "It has the potential to be really important. We have to try to keep up with it, even if it doesn't become the next big thing, because we don't want to miss out on any opportunity to get the word out. If it is the next big thing, we want to be an early adopter."

Transit hubs are among the spots where users of location-based sites are checking in most often. Gowalla, which has 175,000 users in more than 165 countries, reports that its number-one check-in location in Philadelphia is the airport. Foursquare recently partnered with San Francisco's BART [Bay Area Rapid Transit] train service to offer discounts on monthly passes to users who frequently traveled via public transportation, as evidenced by repeated check-ins on the social networking site. Foursquare has implemented a "cheater code" that employs phone GPS [global positioning system] signals to verify that users are where they say they are—i.e., that someone isn't "checking in" at a local gym while lounging on his or her couch at home. Foursquare users can opt to keep their check-ins "off the grid"—meaning that his or her locations are kept private, but he or she still earns points toward merit badges and discount offers from third party businesses.

Annoyance vs. Gain

Widespread efforts by businesses to tap into location-based social networking are what will cause many consumers to tire of the trend, warns Wharton marketing professor Peter Fader. "There's a really good analogy here to e-mail marketing. Fifteen years ago, you got your first e-mail from a company saying, 'Here are this week's specials chosen just for you,' and you said, 'This is cool' and 'How do they know what I wanted?' You read it, you maybe even bought something," he notes. "Maybe the second or third time it was still kind of cool, but then you got totally burned out with it and annoyed."

Fader expects that, just as companies were eager to establish a presence on Facebook and Twitter, the same will be true for location-based social networking. "You've got a zillion companies jumping onto Facebook, posting ads, getting nothing for it and saying, 'Well, this is bad' and then they never do it again. My point is they jumped in too quickly and they gave up too early." He suggests that many businesses expect too much out of social media efforts and that those who use Foursquare—or Twitter or Facebook—as part of an integrated marketing strategy and in a way that makes sense for the brand, will gain the most bang for their buck.

In the midst of rumors last week [in April 2010] that Yahoo may buy Foursquare for $100 million [it did not], the site's creators are still figuring out what type of revenue model would be most profitable. Co-founder Selvadurai notes that the most natural fit would be charging venues for advertising blasts or offers of special discounts to frequent visitors. "A lot of the specials that you see—the venue specials and the 'mayor' specials—were actually suggested by the venues themselves. Venues found out that customers were using Foursquare. They wanted to tap into that and reward them."

Location-based sites work best when partnered with businesses that naturally lend themselves to social interaction and community, such as coffee shops, theaters and hair salons.

But Bradlow cautions that charging businesses to bring ads to users has the potential to overload location-based social networking sites to the point that many customers will stop paying attention. He suggests a model in which Foursquare or another location-based site would earn a portion of revenue for purchases made in connection with promotional partnerships with other companies. "I think firms gravitate toward [social networking] because of—I won't say fear—but the feeling that, 'We've got to be everywhere.' That doesn't mean they should do it," he says. "Firms need a valid return on investment for their marketing spending. They should test the impact of location-based marketing, see the click-through rates, and partner with a company to see if people actually purchased anything."

Hosanagar believes that Foursquare and other location-based sites work best when partnered with businesses that naturally lend themselves to social interaction and community, such as coffee shops, theaters and hair salons. "Some consumer experiences are natural and social—the small local businesses are the kinds that embrace this and really do so successfully."

2

Location-Based Social Networking Is Not Attracting Many Users

Sidney Hill

A business and technology journalist, Sidney Hill is a columnist for TechNewsWorld *and heads a marketing communications consulting firm.*

Despite the media fanfare, location-based social networks are not attracting an appreciable number of regular users in comparison to other platforms. For example, the recorded total of weekly "check-ins" for the smartphone app FourSquare, in which users log their visits to businesses and other establishments, is dwarfed by the recorded total of weekly tweets on Twitter. Furthermore, location-based social networking is touted as a way to discover new places, but the top ten visited venues are national chains. And the "badges" and "titles" given to users who frequent certain venues do not always pay off in discounts or special services. Location-based social networks have yet to find the enticements to gain new users.

All the recent news about Facebook—from its founder being named *Time* magazine's Person of the Year to Goldman Sachs placing a US$450 million bet on its future profitability—makes it clear that social networking platforms are hot commodities.

It's also clear, however, that not all social networking platforms are created equal. So, while Facebook continues to attract hordes of new users and piles of cash from investment bankers, platforms such as Foursquare and Gowalla—known generically as "location-based services"—are living a lonelier existence.

Location-based services are still attracting a fair amount of media attention. What they aren't attracting is users—at least not in any appreciable numbers when compared with the likes of Facebook and Twitter—and this failure to connect with the masses could soon force location-based services into extinction.

Few Regular Users

To get an idea of how dire the situation is for these platforms, consider some numbers. To date, only 4 percent of Americans have used a location-based service, and only 1 percent use them as often as once a week, according to Forrester.

When they launched, location-based services promised to take social networking to the next level, by allowing users to "check in" at businesses they patronize frequently—restaurants, coffee shops, stores, etc. Checking in is supposed to allow your online friends to know where you are, and perhaps entice them to join you for some real-world socializing. It's also supposed to give people a way of discovering exciting new places to shop and mingle by tracking where their friends are checking in.

That pitch earned these sites a good amount of media coverage and a fair number of early adopters. Now, however, the luster associated with location-based services is waning, and it's largely because that early vision of extending virtual social networks into the real world has not materialized.

In the final week of 2010—specifically from December 26 to January 2—the top 10 venues frequented by Foursquare users recorded a total of slightly more than 926,000 check-ins, according to Trendrr, a social media business intelligence service that compiles a weekly tally of Foursquare check-ins for publication on *Advertising Age*.

I contacted Matt Carmichael, director of information projects at *Advertising Age*, to confirm that the figures reflected check-ins across the entire country, and not just in selected metropolitan areas. When Carmichael said they were indeed national figures, my doubts about the future viability of location-based services deepened.

It's . . . easy to see why even some people who describe themselves as avid social media users are questioning the value of location-based services.

The Top 10 Foursquare Venues

The top 10 locations could muster only 926,000 check-ins for an entire week? Twitter records more than 65 million tweets every single day.

A quick look at the top 10 Foursqaure venues also blows holes in the theory that location-based services will help people find exciting new places to visit. Every venue on the list is a national chain—starting with Starbucks, which recorded 146,865 check-ins for the week.

Barnes & Noble attracted 10,416 Foursquare enthusiasts to earn the 10th spot on the list. Sprinkled in between were Target, Wal-Mart, McDonald's, the Apple Store, Best Buy, Burger King, Costco and Ikea.

It's easy to see why people aren't tossing aside their keyboards and rushing out to meet their friends at these places. It's also easy to see why even some people who describe themselves as avid social media users are questioning the value of location-based services.

"I'm a compulsive user of Foursquare, but I have to admit I'm not completely sure why I'm doing it," Neil McIntosh, editor of *The Wall Street Journal*'s European website confessed while interviewing Dennis Crowley, a Foursquare cofounder.

Crowley responded that Foursquare, when used properly, could be considered the digital equivalent of a loyalty card, allowing users to earn discounts or free goods and services at businesses they patronize on a regular basis.

Badges and Titles Are Worthless

There's a major flaw in that theory, however, and it's one of several reasons I think Foursquare and its peers can't last for the long term—at least not without making some major changes.

Foursquare's big shortcoming is this: It gives users badges for checking into particular venues a certain number of times. It even declares the Foursquare user who checks into a venue the most the "mayor" of that location.

If you go on the Foursquare site, you'll learn that mayor of a certain location is supposed to be entitled to special services and discounts from that business. The problem is, in most cases, Foursquare has neglected to let the business owner in on the game—meaning its badges and titles, no matter how lofty they sound, are completely worthless.

I found myself literally laughing out loud while reading a recent letter to an advice column in *Wired* magazine in which a Foursquare user wanted to know if it was OK to ask the owner of a local cafe for some freebies after having "spent a fortune" to become mayor of that location.

The user was advised to tread lightly for fear of being transformed from "that nice guy who's always here to that pushy guy whose sense of entitlement deserves its own ZIP code."

If Foursquare operated its business properly, its users wouldn't have to fear being labeled at all. Foursquare would figure out a way to work out deals with merchants beforehand to ensure that its badges, titles, and whatever it decided to bestow on its members had some real value.

The Right Mix of Enticements

Carmichael, the *Advertising Age* project director, stated it another way: "Location-based services need to figure out the right mix of enticements for the users if they're going to achieve the kind of wide audience and habit-forming behavior needed to succeed. Simply sharing your whereabouts probably won't do it. Connecting consumers and savings will be the key."

This sounds like a fairly simple formula, and one that Crowley said Foursquare was starting to use. Still, there are two reasons it may be too late for this particular form of social networking to really catch on.

First, most technology trends can only support one or two major players. In the social networking realm, Facebook and Twitter already have captured those spots, with Google and Apple looking like the most-likely candidates to move in if one of the top two should falter.

Second, Facebook and Twitter have started adding location-based features of their own, and Facebook in particular understands the dynamics of forming partnerships with businesses. That's a skill the operators of platforms like Foursquare and Gowalla have yet to locate—and unless they do so quickly, they will find them banished from the circle of real social media players.

3

Location-Based Social Networking May Not Be Practical in Some Cities

Zachary Pincus-Roth

Zachary Pincus-Roth is the arts and culture editor for LA Weekly, *the weekly magazine of the* Los Angeles Times *newspaper.*

Designed to encourage users to spontaneously meet with friends, location-based social networks may not be ideally suited for car-dependent cities. For instance, in Los Angeles, a sprawling, traffic-congested metropolis, it can be difficult for a user to join a friend who "checked in" at a venue just a few miles away. Moreover, unlike with traveling on foot, using mobile devices while driving is problematic and unsafe. Nonetheless, some users in driving cities have tailored location-based social networks to fit their social lives, such as coordinating meet-ups and check-ins ahead of time and using the apps as a journal to record their activities.

In early May [2010], Mark Ghuneim was sitting in his hotel room at the Four Seasons near Beverly Hills. He discovered, via his iPhone's Foursquare app, that a friend was at the Echo, a concert venue in Echo Park about eight miles away, about to watch a concert. "I'm realizing that even if I got in my car and drove there right now, I'd miss the set," he said.

At that moment, Ghuneim did not find Foursquare as useful as some of its 1 million users do. Location-based services are the hot new form of social networking, allowing users to tell their friends where they are and what they think of that place. Loopt has more than 3 million users and MyTown has more than 2 million, while Twitter and Google also have location-based features.

But as Ghuneim discovered, these services might not be an ideal fit for Los Angeles, a city that has always had anxiety when it comes to locations. Angelenos tend to spend too much time in a location we don't want to be, driving to a location we're trying to reach, along with a bunch of other people fighting to do the same. The city's spread-out geography and car dependence might make it particularly inhospitable to the spontaneity that these services thrive on.

Better for Walking Cities

For the uninitiated, here's how location-based services work: When you arrive at, say, a bar, you can click on an app on your iPhone or other mobile device to "check in" at that bar. Your friends can see that you're there, so that they might come meet you. Sometimes people leave location-specific tips, such as "the mac and cheese is amazing" or "for stronger drinks, ask the bartender who looks like Kate Beckinsale." Some services make the process into a game—on Foursquare you can earn badges or become "mayor" of a place, while My-Town allows people to "buy" a place and collect virtual rent.

In Manhattan, when your friend has checked in to a bar, she's not more than a half-hour cab ride away at most and often as little as a 10-minute walk. In Los Angeles, the equivalent meet-up might involve a 45-minute drive through traffic, not to mention 10 more minutes looking for parking.

"On balance, stuff like this works better in walking cities," says Sam Altman, chief executive of Silicon Valley-based Loopt. "It's easier to have these spontaneous interactions."

Dennis Crowley, co-founder of Foursquare, told *New York* magazine that his service is "designed to work in New York, and then we kind of tweak it so it works everywhere else. I think it works best in really dense urban areas." (Crowley did not return e-mails asking for comment.)

Useful figures on which cities use these services the most are hard to come by, especially since some areas are simply more populated or tech-savvy than others. On the Austin, Texas-based Gowalla, which has a quarter of a million users, the cities with the most traffic are San Francisco, New York and Austin, with Los Angeles in the next tier, says Josh Williams, the company's chief executive. [Gowalla shut down in March 2012.] On Brightkite, which has 1.5 million monthly users, the top four cities are New York, Los Angeles, San Francisco and Chicago in that order.

Mobile devices are harder to use while driving than while on foot.

Back to Ghuneim, a married man in his 40s who heads a digital marketing agency and, through his frequent check-ins on Foursquare, has become "mayor" of places such as Book Soup in Los Angeles and the Museum of Modern Art in New York. One week after his failed concert outing in Los Angeles, where he was visiting on business, he was back in his West Village apartment. Three music-obsessed friends had checked in at the Mercury Lounge across town in the Lower East Side, where they were about to see the indie band the Joy Formidable. "The band is always going to be 10 minutes late—no problem," he recalls thinking. He hopped in a cab and made the set.

Timing, Spacial Proximity, and Travel Time

Lee Humphreys, an assistant professor of communication at Cornell University, has studied Dodgeball, a primitive predecessor to Foursquare that Crowley also helped found before selling it to Google, where it died out. Humphreys discovered that when your friend checks in to a location, there are three factors that determine whether you redirect your evening to meet them. One is timing—right after work is better than at, say, 11 a.m. The others are spatial proximity (how far you are) and travel time (the time that it takes to get there). "In L.A., during rush hour, travel time would really discourage redirection and meeting up," she says. "Having to go a mile or two in rush hour may be crazy."

Humphreys points out that the arrangement of the streets hurts Los Angeles as well. In New York, if you're heading from Chelsea to Murray Hill, for instance, you can go west on 23rd Street and up 3rd Avenue, or you can go up 8th Avenue and east on 34th Street—whichever will allow you to meet a friend for a drink on the way. But in Los Angeles, sometimes you can take only that dastardly 405. "You might have routinized pathways, but you can still change them and get where you need to be without too much additional time," Humphreys says of New York, whereas in Los Angeles, "there are certain pathways you're meant to travel, and to deviate from them can be difficult."

Another problem is that mobile devices are harder to use while driving than while on foot. California's anti-texting law does not prohibit looking at apps such as Foursquare while driving, but you can't hold the device in your hand and you can't type on it, says Erin Komatsubara, a spokesperson for the California Highway Patrol. "People look at their phones a lot while driving, whether or not they should be, especially on long drives in traffic," says Altman.

David Jarrett, vice president of business development for the Dolce Group, which controls the Hollywood hot spots Geisha House and Les Deux, among others, says he doesn't observe customers using location-based social networking to meet up. "It's more 'I'm here' rather than 'come see me,'" he says. "It's almost like a replacement for a status update on Facebook or Twitter."

Tailoring the Location-Based Experience

Still, all is not lost for location-based services in Los Angeles. Josh Williams, chief executive of Gowalla, which has a quarter of a million users, believes people get used to their city's quirks and tailor their location-based experience accordingly. When he lived in Dallas, the sprawling layout didn't prevent him from meeting up. "I would see people check in and would say, 'Oh, maybe I should go the extra mile and check it out,'" he recalls.

Humphreys found that Dodgeball users in spread-out cities such as Los Angeles, Minneapolis and Seattle were especially likely to "precoordinate" their nights in advance by telling their friends the neighborhood where they'd be partying.

Planning check-ins ahead also helps. Sometimes people will, say, check in at Mel's drive-in as they're stumbling out of the Standard in West Hollywood, so that people will have time to meet up for late-night milkshakes. And if all else fails, good old-fashioned texting can confirm that people actually are where they say they are.

There are even ways to cope with driving. Ford is planning a MyFord Touch feature, which allows for social networking on a dashboard LCD screen. Aha Radio, an app that converts popular apps such as Facebook to a driving-friendly format, is planning to incorporate location-based services. "I'll hear so-and-so checked in with Gowalla a mile ahead at this bar," says Robert Acker, chief executive of Aha Mobile in Palo Alto. "It'll have the ability to map to that location."

Altman even speculates that Los Angeles' sprawling nature might induce citizens to make an extra effort to use these services for meeting up. "I think people really crave face-to-face human connection—that's what we like about location-based technology," he says. "In a very car-focused city, there's less of that, naturally, than in a city like New York where people run into other people all the time."

Plus, of course, these services aren't just used for meeting up. People use them to record their activities, like a diary. Parents use them to keep tabs on their kids. Rob Lawson, chief marketing officer of Brightkite, a location-based service in Burlingame, Calif., with 1.5 million monthly users, notes that some people use these services to stay mentally in touch with their friends. "I may only see you twice a month, but I know where you are the rest of the time," he says. When you do see each other, you can bypass the mundane "What have you been up to?" and instead inquire, "How was Ricky Gervais at the Nokia Theater?"

4

From Apps to Integration: What's Next for Location-Based Services?

Pete Davie

Pete Davie is director of portfolio product management at Tom-Tom, a developer and manufacturer of automotive navigation systems.

The future of location-based services (LBS) is the integration of applications for an enhanced user experience. Currently, these apps are used in a fragmented way, with the user logging on to different ones to perform different tasks throughout the day. With integration, apps will interact seamlessly with less user input. Relevant, convenient content and data based on geographical and calendar information—such as the best available parking or a discount for a favorite restaurant—will be delivered to the user. In the future, navigation services will include more detailed and updated traffic and road information, based on crowdsourcing data from users. Additionally, LBS will be integrated into larger platforms like Facebook and Google.

Today = Apps

Today's meeting is in San Francisco. The address already is in a calendar appointment, so it's easy to cut and paste it from there into my Tom Tom navigation app. Rush hour has passed, so traffic isn't too bad. But on arrival in the city, it takes an extra 15 minutes to find parking, which is charged at a full day rate, even though we're only there for a couple of hours.

A quick search on Yelp to find a coffee shop where we can grab something before the meeting and then a check-in on Foursquare to check for deals (we're a big fan of the Foursquare/AMEX partnership). The meeting runs long, and, by the time we get back to the car, traffic is already backing up heading south. The navigation app re-routes us down 1-280 instead of US-101.

We send a Glympse home, so they know we're running late (much better than texting and driving). We check the Open Table reservation for dinner tonight—should still make it if traffic isn't too bad.

This fairly typical day used at least five location-specific apps, in addition to all the other daily use apps (e-mail, calendar, SMS, weather, Facebook, Twitter, etc.).

Tomorrow = Integration

Now imagine a similar day with an advanced smart-phone operating system (OS), where interaction among apps is seamless to the user.

The alarm goes off automatically based on the calendar schedule. In fact, it's 30 minutes earlier than originally planned because of rain and fog on the Peninsula—a reminder to leave early because of traffic. The colleague we're meeting in San Francisco is a Twitter addict, so we'll just get the phone to update his Twitter-feed if we're running late.

We get to the city and get routed to a parking lot with available spaces—our calendar shows we're only in the city for a couple of hours, so we get a special fixed rate. We pay directly on the near-field communication (AIFC)-enabled phone and don't have to wait in any lines or find change for the machine.

We end up grabbing lunch at a Thai place we've been to before—they see we're in San Francisco and send a coupon for that day. One click, and a lunch reservation is confirmed. Another alert on the way home tells us the wireless router we looked at online was on special at the Best Buy right next to the freeway, so we reroute and grab that on the way home. Traffic is terrible, but automatic updates to Facebook keep the family up-to-date.

These changes will have a profound impact on the way location content, services and applications are created and delivered.

Much of the underlying technology to support this already exists today, but it's not seamlessly integrated into the OS. All of this can happen with little direct user interaction—based on calendar and location information, relevant data and content can be pushed to users in an integrated, easy-to-consume way.

Where We're Headed

Although location-based services (LBSs) are increasingly ubiquitous, they're still in the early stages of evolution. Global smartphone penetration is less than 10 percent today; as this continues to increase, LBSs will evolve and become increasingly sophisticated.

In addition, today's LBS ecosystem is very fragmented: we check-in using Foursquare, we look for reviews on Yelp, and we navigate using TomTom. Apps such as Glympse fill niche gaps in the LBS ecosystem. Smartphone OSs and platforms such as Facebook are evolving, and user interfaces (UIs) are becoming more customized and personalized.

Apps and developers will continue to drive innovation, but the focus will be on core functionality and the ability to integrate into an overall UI experience. People will still check in, search for reviews and navigate, and the underlying technologies will continue to evolve, but the UI experience will be integrated at the OS and platform level. These changes will have a profound impact on the way location content, services and applications are created and delivered.

Content

In the future, we'll see content (maps) evolve away from traditional delivery models to always-connected services. Static content delivered in exchange file formats won't be acceptable. Organizations won't invest in development teams to compile location content and solve complex problems such as routing and navigation.

Location will be a feature in a larger solution in many of the emerging LBS use cases. Developers will depend on content providers to deliver content in an accessible, easy-to-consume way. In many cases, this will mean delivery via application programming interfaces (APIs) on a hosted developer platform.

It also could mean the delivery of run-time maps such as Navigation Data Standard (NDS) directly to original equipment manufacturers (OEMs)—although NDS is being developed primarily as an automotive standard, it also could be used for mobile and LBS solutions. In both cases, content providers deliver content as well as the services that incorporate the content. Examples include rendered map tiles, geocoding services and routing algorithms.

As more devices are connected, a logical extension of the content model . . . is to incorporate live services in addition to core map content.

Fresh Maps

An inherent advantage to these new delivery models is that it will become easier for content providers to deliver fresher, more up-to-date (and ultimately live) content. As data-collection tools become more sophisticated, map edits can be made in almost real time and then pushed to application developers through new product-delivery mechanisms.

In turn, as more experiences take place on mobile, connected devices, applications can be continuously updated. This means the user experience is vastly improved—users expect their maps to reflect reality and incorporate new roads quickly. This can be turned into a closed loop as input provided by users (actively and passively) then can be delivered back to content providers to be incorporated into databases (i.e., crowdsourcing).

Services

Although the ubiquity of LBS is good news for content providers, it also created a (perceived) view that basic map content is becoming commoditized at the user level. In fact, it's clear that building and maintaining high-quality maps requires significant investment, and those costs still have to be covered directly (through licensing) or indirectly (through advertising). As more devices are connected, a logical extension of the content model—from revenue and value perspectives—is to incorporate live services in addition to core map content.

Real-time traffic is the most obvious and highest value of these services. Today's traffic services work well on major roads and in major markets; the next step in this evolution is to scale to include all roads everywhere. There are several components to this:

1. The creation of open location referencing systems (e.g., TomTom's OpenLR standard) that can tie traffic information to any map anywhere.

2. The ability to fuse multiple sources of traffic information, including crowdsourced data.

3. The development of an ecosystem that can manage and deliver live content across devices and machines, including smartphones, personal navigation devices (PNDs), connected cars, road sensors and variable-message signs (VMSs).

In addition to real-time traffic, new services include local search (eventually reducing the dependency on "on-device" points of interest), weather, fuel price, parking and event information. All these services will create potential direct and, more likely, indirect revenue streams to complement traditional map-license revenue. Their success will depend on how easily they integrate into broader applications, from technical and business perspectives.

Successful companies will be those that most easily and deeply integrate content, services and applications into this developing ecosystem.

Applications

Applications in the LBS ecosystem can include everything from off-board and on-board turn-by-turn navigation systems to niche apps like Glympse and Foursquare to integration into larger ecosystems such as Facebook and Google. As cloud computing and connectivity become cheaper and more accessible, more apps will be off-board or hybrid. Although there still will be a place for "reference apps," success will be driven by the underlying technology and how easily it integrates into large ecosystems.

Monetization and Future Trends

The LBS market is expected to grow from less than $3 billion in 2010 to more than $10 billion by 2015. Content and service providers, app developers, operators and OEMs all will be competing for this revenue.

To date, navigation applications have generated most of that revenue, but this will increasingly be replaced by local search. Mobile advertising still is in a nascent stage, but it's already clear that users will act on mobile ads much more immediately, so click-to-call and click-to-navigate ads are effective. To put this in perspective, Google reported mobile revenue of $2.5 billion—almost all ad driven—in 2011.

One of the missing pieces that's key to building out the LBS ecosystem is support for mobile payments. As NFC, Google Wallet and other alternatives become ubiquitous, this will create a closed loop for advertisers, where buying decisions can be followed all the way from the ad or promotion to the point of sale.

An important implication of such for-content providers will be the demand for pedestrian and indoor content to enable routing to the point of sale, plus the associated positioning technologies required as alternatives to GPS. Indoor content initially will take the form of higher-level mall and airport maps, but eventually more-detailed aisle-by-aisle layouts for major retailers will be available.

Successful companies will be those that most easily and deeply integrate content, services and applications into this developing ecosystem. Companies that can offer location and navigation solutions across platforms (e.g., PNDs, Smartphones, OEMs, etc.) as well as easy-to-integrate APIs to deliver specific content and services will be well positioned to realize such success.

5

Location-Based Services Effectively Reach Consumers

David Murphy

David Murphy is publisher of Mobile Marketing Magazine, *a British online publication that covers the mobile marketing industry.*

Location-based social networking offers a valuable opportunity for brands to reach consumers on the go. Geolocation services offered by the likes of Foursquare and Facebook enable businesses to offer "real-time" rewards to customers who "check in" on a regular basis. In addition, businesses can use "geofencing" to target consumers near places that are relevant to their products. Small businesses are early adopters of location-based advertising, gaining access to a market available only through conventional ads, and average click-through rates for location-based campaigns are higher than other forms of mobile and online advertising. Therefore, big brands reluctant to use location-based social networking are highly advised to employ the service.

Anyone who uses Twitter can't have failed to notice that for some social networkers at least, life seems to be turning into one big game.

'I just unlocked the adventurer badge!'. . .

'I just became the mayor of the Dog & Duck in Hampstead!' These people, of course, are using Foursquare, the social-networking service that rewards users for visiting,

David Murphy, "Geo-targeting: Location, Location, Location!," *Revolution*, September 16, 2010, p. 44. Reproduced from *Revolution* magazine with the permission of the copyright owner, Haymarket Business Publications Limited.

or in the Foursquare vernacular, 'checking in' at certain places. You visit, you check in via your mobile phone, and whoever registers the most check-ins for any given venue becomes the mayor of that venue, with all the kudos that comes with the title.

So far, so what, you might think. But some people believe that Foursquare has a very interesting business model, because it provides brands with the potential to start offering their own 'real-time' rewards to consumers who check in to their retail outlets regularly. So what looks at first glance like a bit of fun suddenly becomes a pretty sophisticated, location-based loyalty tool. It gets even better when you add in the user-generated element; if there's a venue you visit regularly that's not listed on Foursquare, just add it yourself.

It's clever stuff, and it is starting to gain some traction. Every Wednesday, for example, the mayor of each Domino's Pizza franchise across the UK is rewarded with a free small pizza, while any Foursquare user who checks in and spends over pounds 10 gets a free garlic pizza bread. Starbucks is also offering Foursquare rewards in the US. But aside from these isolated examples, it's fair to say that most brands don't seem to have got their heads around Foursquare in particular, and location-based services in general, just yet. Which begs the question: why not?

Social-media strategist Andrew Grill identifies two reasons why brands have been slow to get Foursquare. He says: 'It has an amazing back-end system, but it doesn't have enough sales or business development people to go out there and sell the proposition. On the other side of things, brands and agencies don't get it yet, because the people who make the buying decisions have only just started to understand Facebook and Twitter.'

Big Brands

Foursquare is not the only service finding out the hard way that it takes time to get big brands on board. Facebook Places, a rival geolocation service, is yet to get off the ground. However, Geocast, which works with mobile internet and app publishers to deliver location-aware advertising to UK mobile-phone users, is gaining traction. Its system enables advertisers to target consumers who come within a specified distance, whether that's 100 metres or five miles, of a certain location. While early users of the service tended to target consumers who were near one of their outlets, many now also choose to target people when they approach one of their competitors. Much of the advertising is offer-led, enticing consumers to visit a nearby store with the promise of a 10 per cent discount.

One of the reasons bigger brands have not yet tapped into the power of location-based advertising is because of a disconnect between mobile advertising and digital marketing managers within large companies.

Chief executive Brad Liebmann says Geocast has around 10,000 advertisers, the majority of which are shops or restaurants. But he concedes that most of these are small, independent traders, rather than national multiples.

'Smaller businesses tend to be the first to catch on to the power of local advertising, and they are also the ones with the least number of alternatives available to them, because local media is dying,' he says.

Such businesses are beginning to realise the Geocast technology works very nicely for them. Husband and wife team Ian and Sally Selves run a mobile tyre-replacement business called IDS in Halifax. Customers book appointments to have tyres replaced and the couple visit them on their premises and carry out the work. IDS has been using Geocast to generate leads within West Yorkshire for the past 12 months and, according to Sally Selves, it now contributes around 10 to 15 per cent of the company's turnover each month. 'Geocast gives us access to a vast market which we could never afford to cover with conventional advertising and, vitally, we only pay for results,' she says.

Hidden Potential

Liebmann believes that one of the reasons bigger brands have not yet tapped into the power of location-based advertising is because of a disconnect between mobile advertising and digital marketing managers within large companies.

He says: 'Mobile advertising is not most effective for brand building; it should be used to drive footfall in store. But currently, digital marketing managers are tasked with driving traffic to their sites; they do not care about driving footfall—that's someone else's job.'

Liebmann believes it will take a couple of years for this issue to resolve itself, as the penny drops and the digital marketing manager will start to be incentivised by driving footfall as well as web traffic—or the mobile advertising role will be taken over by the person in charge of driving footfall.

Alistair Goodman, chief executive of Placecast in the US, tells a similar story. Placecast puts 'geofences' around places of interest to brands. So for an outdoor activity retailer, this could be their stores, but also ski resorts or country parks with walking and bike trails. Consumers are then invited to opt in to receive targeted text messages called 'ShopAlerts' when they cross one of the geofences. The messages are targeted, based on the consumer's interest, so a mountain biker and walker entering the same area could both be targeted by the same advertiser, but with different messages.

Goodman believes that the medium—SMS [short message service]—is vital to the success of the service. 'We use SMS because it's ubiquitous,' he says. 'We hear a lot about smartphones, but in the US there are still only 21 per cent of consumers who have one, and brands want to reach the largest potential number of consumers.'

Time Lag

Last autumn [in 2009], Placecast conducted research among consumers who had received ShopAlerts from three retailers: American Eagle (youth fashion); REI (outdoor equipment); and Sonic (fast food). The study found that 65 per cent of respondents had made a purchase after receiving a ShopAlert, but interestingly, not all the purchases were instant. While a majority of recipients opened and read the text alert immediately, for those who responded to it, 27 per cent did so within one day, while 35 per cent responded in one to three days.

Advertisers are seeing average click-through rates that are north of 7 per cent, which is fantastic compared to regular mobile or online advertising.

Goodman believes this puts paid to the idea that location-aware mobile advertising is all about offers and discounts. 'One of our advertisers, North Face, has more than 1,000 geofences set up, and it doesn't even do discounts,' says Goodman. 'North Face sees it as a tool to provide value to customers with messaging over the long term, to strengthen the relationship and increase repeat purchasing—it's not all about discounts.'

Like Geocast's Liebmann, Goodman believes big brands will find their way to location-based services. He claims many are discouraged by the nature of the market. 'There are lots of start-ups creating fragmentation, and brands want to work with companies that have a sales force and a proven model with results and analytics they can understand. We will see that ultimately, but it's early days.'

Perhaps they should just give it a try. Back in Europe, David Barker, advertising sales director, Europe and Africa, for Nokia-owned Navteq, says brands that try location-based advertising via its Location Point Advertising (LPA) platform, which it offers to mobile ad networks and app developers, find it works.

'Advertisers are seeing average click-through rates that are north of 7 per cent, which is fantastic compared to regular mobile or online advertising,' he says. 'McDonald's ran a trial in Finland and, at the end of it, said it wanted all the inventory available in that country. We are seeing success; maybe we just need to shout a bit louder about it.'

Best Western Hotels recently ran a location-based campaign targeting German consumers using Nokia Ovi Map-enabled smartphones with ads delivered by Navteq's LPA platform. Ads sent to consumers approaching one of 180 Best Western properties throughout Germany enticed consumers with an offer to receive a 30 per cent discount when the user booked early at a Best Western property. The campaign generated a click-through rate of 1.44 per cent, and 15 per cent of all consumers who clicked on the initial ad requested mapping information to the local Best Western hotel.

'Location-based advertising works because the customer is often travelling and in a place they are not familiar with, so our approach is not so much pure marketing as trying to help them and engage them in a smart way,' says Alexander Birk, ecommerce manager for Best Western Hotels Germany.

Most brands know this location-based stuff makes perfect sense, it's just that, as with anything new, there's a degree of nervousness about who you partner with, and the perennial fear of being seen fixing something that isn't broken.

This approach is also being adopted by many local authorities up and down the country. Liverpool City Council is one example. It offers residents a service that enables them to find out when to put their rubbish out for collection by texting the word 'Bins' plus their house number and postcode to 62233. Thereafter, they get a reminder text each week (unless they opt out) the day before the collection. 'Most people have mobile phones, and text messaging is a great way to find out essential information,' says Liverpool City Council Leader, Joe Anderson.

If you talk to Greq Le Tocq, managing director of Vouchercloud, you could be forgiven for thinking that location-based advertising has already gone through the growing pains, and is as mature and established an advertising medium as the web. The company launched its iPhone app, offering location-based money-off coupons in February, and in the first five months after the launch, saw almost 600,000 app downloads and 250,000 mobile coupon downloads. Le Tocq estimates that Vouchercloud's mobile vouchers saved UK consumers over pounds 1m [million] over the period.

Big-brand Buy-in

What's more impressive is the roster of brands offering mobile coupons via Vouchercloud. The list includes Pizza Hut, Zizzi, Prezzo and Carluccio's. It may have an unfair advantage, as Vouchercloud was borne out of a company that has been publishing hefty, print-based voucher books in cities up and down the UK for many years, so it already had a good relationship with many leading high-street brands, which were looking for a nationwide, more up-to-date coupon offering.

There's a lesson in there somewhere: most brands know this location-based stuff makes perfect sense, it's just that, as with anything new, there's a degree of nervousness about who you partner with, and the perennial fear of being seen fixing something that isn't broken. But with redemption rates as high as nine per cent for two-for-one vouchers, it's clearly time for brands to join the party.

6

Location-Based Services May Not Effectively Reach Consumers

Kathy Cripps

Kathy Cripps is president of the Council of Public Relations Firms, a trade organization representing public relations firms in both the United States and internationally.

Businesses are looking more to location-based social networking as the key to successful mobile advertising. However, several issues present challenges in reaching consumers through platforms like Foursquare, Facebook, and Google. First, consumers are largely unfamiliar with location-based social networking platforms; 60 percent of smartphone owners do not use location-based services, and only 4 percent of adult Internet users use them. Next, concerns over privacy surround location-based services, including the surreptitious collection and leaking of user data. As access to such information widens, businesses must consider the comfort and trust of consumers.

How cool would it be to walk into a hardware store and see advertisements and coupons for exactly the plumbing fixture we're seeking?

Well, it could be cool. Sort of.

The technology for location-based marketing is here, and it isn't all about Foursquare: Facebook's Places and Google's

Latitude let you tell your friends where you are. Facebook has plans to let local businesses market to consumers who come into their establishments; one of Google's most promising businesses at present is location-based advertising. As Google's director of mobile advertising has been quoted, "Location will be one of the cornerstones of mobile advertising. Merging local businesses with mobile [advertising] is very, very important for us."

A Lukewarm Response

Still, location-based marketing has as yet received only a lukewarm response from American consumers. According to one survey, "more than 60% of active smartphone users don't use location-based services; among those non-users, 70% aren't aware of the apps or don't fully understand what they do." The Pew Research Center has found that only 4% of adult Internet users use a location-based service like Foursquare. Globally, there's more adoption: One survey found that "nearly one-quarter of mobile users say they are getting comfortable with ads. Even better, more than one-third of consumers (38 percent) say mobile ads serve 'an important purpose,'" with personalized content (including potentially location-based messaging) most appealing to consumers.

One big concern of American consumers seems to be privacy. In recent months, privacy issues have cast a shadow over the online world as a whole, including location-based services. Google was recently assessed a fine of 100,000 Euros for improperly collecting and keeping data as part of its Street View offering. A study by *The Wall Street Journal* recently showed that mobile apps were leaking large amounts of information without consumers' knowledge. The courts are currently considering whether law enforcement agencies require warrants to obtain location-based records on individuals, and the question that has generated scary headlines in the media, as the *Pittsburgh Post-Gazette* recently informed readers, "Big Brother

Has Access to Devices That Knows Where You Are." All of this and more has led the Obama administration to call for a "Privacy Bill of Rights" covering online consumers, including provisions for location-based services.

In our position as leaders in technology, we need to think through vexing privacy issues right now, proactively, before public policy imperatives are forced onto us by a nervous populace.

It's worth noting that not all Americans are equally concerned about privacy issues. Recent polling of Americans found that more feel they are losing control over their data, yet only a portion of the population feels concerned about that. A little over a third said they "cared less about privacy than five years ago," and about the same said they care more. Participation in social media explains this divergence: "Among active social network users, 58 percent said privacy was less important and only 14 percent said its importance was growing. Non-social media users were almost a mirror image in reverse, with 53 percent saying privacy is more important to them, but only 20 percent saying it was less so."

What About Consumer Comfort and Trust?

As an editorialist in the *Denver Post* has written, "Location-based services will grow in popularity as people become more comfortable with them. We hope users will be savvy about something as sensitive as one's physical location, just as they ought to be with other personal information." We should add that companies and firms are well advised to think carefully about the privacy implications of their marketing tactics, both as a matter of principle and to obtain the best result.

Lines between the marketing disciplines have eroded more than ever before, and public relations firms are finding themselves on the forefront of technology. Increasingly, we are gaining access to consumer data, a development that allows us to fine-tune our messaging better and offer more consumer value. But what about consumer comfort and trust with the brands? Just because we have technological capability doesn't mean we should use it in a haphazard manner. In our position as leaders in technology, we need to think through vexing privacy issues right now, proactively, before public policy imperatives are forced onto us by a nervous populace.

It's not just consumers that must be ready for location-based marketing. We need to be, too.

7

Retailers May Benefit from Geofencing

Alliance Data

Based in Plano, Texas, Alliance Data is a loyalty program and data marketing company.

Geofencing is a form of location-based advertising in which a retailer sends a text-based promotion to consumers who have opted in to receive communications from the said retailer. A message is texted to consumers who are in the store's vicinity or targeted location. Unlike traditional advertising, it enables businesses to deliver pertinent messages to consumers at the most opportune place and time. In fact, in a 2012 pilot program, more than a third of participating consumers made transactions after receiving texts from retailers. Also, in a post-program survey, more than a third of respondents reported that the texts influenced their buying choices and 84 percent felt at ease with communicating with retailers on their mobile devices. Best practices for geofencing include gaining permission from consumers first and sending texts that are well timed and respectful.

Last year [in 2012], holiday shoppers in Columbus, Ohio, kicked off a new trend in marketing as their favorite brands tried a more personalized tactic for reaching customers.

Amid the bustling crowds and noise of the busiest shopping season of the year, these early adopters received a special offer via text message from several stores at the Easton Town Center mall. The difference from other text-based promotions? These messages were location-aware, and only triggered when the shopper was within a short walk of participating retailers. The test program proved tremendously effective, encouraging visits, boosting brand awareness, and showcasing a promising new concept: *location-based marketing.*

Geofencing: The Broadest Reach

Alliance Data spearheaded the five-week test of geofencing, an emerging channel for delivering these tailored, location-based messages through digital devices. We chose geofencing over other technologies (GPS or Wi-Fi, for example) because it afforded us the broadest reach—anyone, regardless of their cellular phone or service, was able to participate. By sending targeted texts to their phones only when customers were in the store's vicinity, the program was more selective than traditional tactics that are disconnected from a shopper's location. The pilot, supported by Alliance Data's mobile marketing platform and strategic partner backing, proved that—when done right—geofencing is more affordable and easier to implement than many may realize. And success in the mall environment only hints at the larger possibilities: hotels, casinos, sporting events, zoos, amusement parks, and universities could all benefit from geofenced promotional programs, to name just a few. With location-based marketing, brands can deliver a simple, hard-to-resist pitch that boils down to: "*You're nearby. Here's something just for you. Come engage with us!*"

Mobile technology offers fast-evolving opportunities for shrewd marketers. Smartphones and tablets aren't just growing in popularity, they're becoming a necessity. Almost half of Americans now have mobile Internet access, and these devices have become constant companions—they are the first screen many look at when they get up in the morning and the last one they check when they go to bed. Consider the behavior of folks between the ages of 18 and 34, for instance: three quarters of men and nearly two thirds of women in this youthful demographic check their phones every hour. Young people aren't alone, either; demographics of almost all ages are hooked on their devices.

No one wants a flood of useless and trivial texts to greet them when they enter the mall or the airport, for instance. Send too many messages, and brands can do more harm than good.

With the mobile economy here to stay—and the cost of ignoring it unrecoverable—location-based communications are a very attractive next step in marketing. Geofencing technology enables timely, relevant and powerful messages to modern consumers at the right place, at the right time, and in the right way.

Best Practices

Here's how geofencing works: When customers enter a targeted geographic area during a specified time, they receive triggered messages on their mobile devices urging them to take advantage of a special offer. Marketers define the location and size of the geofenced zone through cellular towers or Wi-Fi signals, and communications are delivered via text messages, emails, or notifications from branded apps.

Messages don't go to every mobile phone user within that geofence, of course. According to standard industry protocol, recipients must opt in to geofencing programs twice—first giving permission to receive messages on their devices and then to receive location-based communications. Once permissions are granted, program managers must treat the privilege with savvy timing and respect for the customer. No one wants a flood of useless and trivial texts to greet them when they enter the mall or the airport, for instance. Send too many messages, and brands can do more harm than good. And clumsy, too—specific messages might make people feel like Big Brother is watching them.

The Easton geofencing pilot program took a less-is-more approach. No more than one message was sent to a shopper in any five-day period, and no shopper received more than four messages throughout the campaign. The program also kept communications general: messages would note a customer's arrival at Easton, then offer her a chance to win a $5,000 shopping spree at one of the participating stores (including Express, The Limited, Pier 1 imports, and Pottery Barn). Sure, there's technology that can pinpoint the exact location of mobile users—right down to the boutique they just walked into—but it's far better to use a softer, less precise message.

Geofencing also is simpler and more affordable than many think. Locaid, Alliance Data's partner on the Easton pilot program, can put up a virtual fence in a matter of hours using cellular towers. There are costs associated with each ping and message; Alliance Data mitigates the majority of these costs for clients. And smart operators can reduce costs further by focusing on key dates (Black Friday, for instance) and keeping communications tight and relevant. During the Easton program, Alliance Data sent just over 700 messages, which broke down to less than two messages per participating shopper. Yet that relatively small number yielded impressive results.

Laying the Groundwork for Success

Prior to launching the pilot program, Alliance Data sent introductory emails to cardholders of several branded programs. If they agreed to accept location-based text messages, they were eligible to win the shopping spree. Just one person took home that prize, but participating retailers benefited in several ways.

More than a third of participants made transactions following triggered messages; in turn, those sales were more than anticipated. Overall, participants spent more on their cards than forecasted—up 4.9 percent on Black Friday and up 2.5 percent during the entire holiday shopping season.

A post-campaign survey further detailed the positive impact. More than a third of respondents indicated the text messages influenced their purchase decisions, while nearly three-quarters agreed that mobile campaigns can influence customers' decisions to visit stores. What's more, most welcomed the tailored messages: 84 percent were comfortable using their phones to communicate with retailers; 60 percent said they had no privacy or security concerns.

Location-based marketing has the potential to turn mobile users into devoted consumers. In the post-campaign survey, 68 percent indicated they likely would sign up for future location-based text messages. If relevant and respectful, such communications can connect with consumers in a personal, one-on-one way, like a high-tech, virtual version of the traditional face-to-face interaction between a loyal customer and a brand representative.

Just the Beginning

Geofencing shouldn't be considered a one-off program. Instead, it works best as part of a multi-platform; multi-screen marketing plan involving mobile, websites, apps, credit and loyalty cards, in-store and online communications, and more. Together, these pieces can pay big dividends with customers by increasing revenue and vitalizing a brand's image. For instance, 61 percent of people have a better opinion of brands when they offer good digital experiences.

8

Geofencing Can Be an Invasion of Privacy

Matt Silk

Matt Silk, CMO, leads operations for sales and marketing, corporate development and strategic partnerships for Waterfall Mobile (www.waterfallmobile.com).

Geofencing, or the use of location-based services to send tailored text alerts to consumers in close proximity to a retail store or other property, raises privacy concerns. Constantly monitoring the whereabouts of consumers is not only expensive but is intrusive. The use of real-time location data to reach consumers on their mobile devices is highly personal; just one annoying or invasive text alert can drive away customers. If a marketer uses geofencing, consumers should control when and where they can be contacted and how much information they share. Brand managers must also be sure the opt-in and opt-out protocol is clear and allows users to report abuse.

L ocation-based services are getting an enormous amount of attention lately, with the launch of Google's Near Me Now for mobile and other high-profile announcements. As a mobile executive, I am thrilled that this idea—once literally the stuff of science fiction—is finally coming together. But as a mobile consumer, I have the same concern as everyone else: privacy. I want to know that any messaging I receive is opt-in only; that I will only be contacted when and how I want to be; and that whatever communications come my way will be 100% spam free.

One of the hot new areas of mobile marketing is "geofencing," or the idea of tracking people on a mobile subscriber list based on proximity to a particular retail store, and then sending out tailored messaging alerts. It sounds great in theory, but I just can't get behind it. Geofencing involves knowing the location of individual customers at all times so you can "ping" them anytime they are physically near individual stores.

Constantly tracking and watching where consumers are would involve checking location every few minutes. That could get ridiculously expensive (carrier lookups for messaging, draining your battery for smartphones, etc.) and feels a little too big brother for me. It's like an electronic dog collar that buzzes every time I hit the fence.

[Mobile devices] are more sacred and personal to their owners, and if marketers cross the privacy lines with mobile marketing, consumers won't let them off the hook so easily.

Not to mention the fact that, if you are looking to hit someone with a message every time that person gets within a certain distance of your store, then you need to be constantly ready to provide engaging content. National retail chains are already buried trying to track all of the different channels where their customers are with the social-media explosion. Are they really ready to sign up for this task? I don't think they have the staff or budget to deliver on the hype that is being marketed.

Inherently, and Extremely, Personal

Here is a great and simple use case for location that makes sense to me. Let's say your mobile list has 20,000 people on it and you want to send a marketing message on Wednesday at 3 p.m. Eastern Time. At the appointed time, do one check on location, and then ping everyone within a set distance of those stores—with a highly relevant message. Everyone else on the subscriber list will get a different message, with a generic, non-location-based coupon offer. You could have 50 different messages each targeting specific locations.

Real-time location data is inherently, and extremely, personal. Brands should respect this access and never abuse it— lest it be taken away, either by the user or by wireless carriers. A rule of thumb that applies to all digital messaging, and particularly applies here, is this: if you don't have something compelling to say, don't text your customers. If they get annoyed and reply "STOP" to a text, then that customer is gone forever.

Let users have the option to choose when and where you can contact them and to divulge as much or as little information as they want. This ensures your contact is relevant and desired. Give them clear options to select from when they are setting up their profiles. If people want to input their sex, age, gender, marital status, time of day to contact, number of messages, give them that option.

Any brand manager pondering an LBS program should walk through the opt-in and -out protocol personally. If the rules aren't extremely clear, consider a redesign. Whatever that costs, it's better than the potential blowback of a mobile campaign gone awry. A process should also be in place to allow for users to report abuse of their information and a way to have reports handled in a timely matter.

In many ways, this is the same set of rules that marketers should be following on the web—but not all of them do. Consumers, rather than making brands pay for that privacy breach, are more apt to just delete the email and move on. Mobile phones are different. They are more sacred and personal to their owners, and if marketers cross the privacy lines with mobile marketing, consumers won't let them off the hook so easily.

9

How Smartphones Are the New Wingman

Heather Kelly

Heather Kelly is a technology writer and producer for CNN.com.

Mobile dating applications that use location data to find available, nearby singles are bringing spontaneity to online dating. While profile-based dating sites involve browsing, filtering, and screening potential mates before meeting, location-based dating apps have proven popular for those with a desire to connect on a whim and with gay men, for whom finding dates can be a challenge. These apps do have a reputation for promiscuity and raise security and privacy concerns, particularly with the exploitation of minors. But many people sign on just to socialize—and to bring them back into the real world of dating.

Malia checks Blendr, the location-based networking app, on her phone six or seven times a day, sorting through messages from strangers who know she's in their vicinity and responding only to the ones who don't seem creepy.

Though she is surrounded by people in Los Angeles, the 23-year-old waitress finds that her smartphone is still helpful for meeting new friends or potential romances.

"I catch happy hours with people, meet friends, maybe go on dates here and there," explained the woman, who asked that her last name not be used. "You meet a lot of people who are very spontaneous."

Online dating used to be largely a deskbound activity. But in recent years, mobile apps like Blendr have employed constant Internet access and location-based services to turn the smartphone into a wingman of sorts. Phones now give singles the ability to find someone who's available, and nearby, at a moment's notice, bringing a bit of serendipity back to the Internet dating scene.

Profile-based dating sites such as Match.com and eHarmony suffer from a courtship delay. After you open an account, much of your time is spent browsing and filtering—tentatively messaging strangers, screening them on the phone and over e-mail and instant message before finally setting up coffee dates with the few deemed worthy. This extra caution is probably smart, but it discourages spontaneity and leaves almost too much time to rule people out based on picky details.

Proximity in Common

But today's mobile location apps, which work with a phone's built-in GPS [global positioning system], connect lovelorn singles who have something more urgent in common: proximity.

The gay community was first to recognize the potential for location-based networking. The popular gay-meet-up app Grindr was released in 2009. Grindr taps into the smartphone's location information to show to-the-point profiles of men in a certain radius who are available to meet.

"Grindr solves a very big problem in the lives of gay men," explained Grindr chief executive Joel Simkhai. "How do I find other gay men?"

The app has been a global success, with 1.1 million daily active users in 192 countries (that means just four countries don't have at least one person on Grindr).

With a few tweaks—beefed-up privacy settings, expanded profiles—Grindr then rolled out Blendr for straight singles. The straight app hasn't been as huge of a hit just yet (though it's doing especially well in Australia).

For all these apps, divulging sensitive information like a GPS location raises serious security concerns, such as the potential for stalking or worse.

OkCupid, one of the hipper, younger-oriented dating services, also made its own location-aware app last year called OkCupid Local. Users can find people nearby who are on the service, and the app recommends potential dates by using data users provide when filling out extensive profiles.

Match.com and eHarmony have also gone mobile, but their apps are still more like window shopping—flipping through profiles and judging the ratio of wit to sincerity, seeing what the algorithm has to say about your chances of hitting it off—than finding a potential romance in the coffeeshop down the street.

Other startups have recognized that the desire to meet new people isn't limited to dating. Highlight shows mini-profiles of people, including friends and strangers, around you on a map. Ban.jo pinpoints nearby people who are in your existing social networks, including Twitter, Facebook and Foursquare.

Serious Security and Privacy Concerns

For all these apps, divulging sensitive information like a GPS location raises serious security concerns, such as the potential for stalking or worse. In July, social-networking app Skout had to ban minors after three men were accused of sexually assaulting children they met through the service. The Skout service for 13- to 17-year-olds was suspended.

There are privacy concerns as well. People are frequently unaware of just how much identifying information they post on the Internet by checking into social networks and sharing photos whose metadata reveal where they were taken. As with going to a bar and talking to the first stranger you find with decent hair, people should use caution.

While location-based dating apps have a reputation of being just for people who want to hook up, users say they're increasingly using them for more G-rated purposes: to make friends. According to Grindr's internal research, members make one to five new platonic friends though the app.

Simkhai fires up Grindr when he's in a new country to get restaurant recommendations and other tips from locals. Malia met one of her closest friends on Blendr and will sign on during trips to Vegas just to network, she said.

Fitting Well with the Moment

Location data isn't required to make the smartphone useful for meeting people. Phones also facilitate a longstanding challenge of courtship: the exchange of numbers. Instead of scribbling digits on a soggy cocktail napkin, smartphone owners can use Bump, a mobile app that lets you exchange contact information easily by bumping two phones together. Bump was an early hit in the iPhone app store and has been downloaded more than 100 million times.

"It fits very well with that moment where you're nervous and want to meet someone new but don't know how how to approach them and ask for a number," said Bump CEO [chief executive officer] Dave Lieb, who believes his app turns the act of bumping phones into a flirty, fun act.

The Internet gave birth to some great helpers for shy people looking for love—chatrooms, dating sites, instant messaging, missed connections posts on Craigslist. But the new generation of dating tools appeals to people who think of dating as an active, spur-of-the-moment pursuit that takes place in the fluid world of bars, parties and other social settings.

10

Location-Based Social Networking Can Enable Stalking

Lisa Riordan Seville

Lisa Riordan Seville is a reporter based in Brooklyn, New York.

Geotagging technology, which enables friends and family to keep up with each other's whereabouts in real-time, is the next big thing in social networking. But many users unknowingly leave a digital trail that can make them vulnerable to stalking. Controversial sites that expose sensitive information from location-based social networks have even been launched to educate the public about the dangers. However, privacy settings for these networks are confusing and complex, and privacy laws for electronic data remain unclear. Moving into legal gray areas, law enforcement has already begun collecting and storing information about citizens from location-based services, equipped with the technology to track a person throughout the day.

In the world of social networking, Carri Bugbee is hardly a novice. The Portland, Oregon social media marketing strategist has 7,164 followers on Twitter, 1,197 Facebook friends and more than 500 connections on LinkedIn. But when she got involved with geotagging through a location-based network, she received an uncomfortable wake-up call.

Literally. One evening last February [in 2009], she used foursquare, the popular location-based mobile network, to "check in" at a local restaurant, letting friends know where she was sitting down to dinner. Then she got a call on the restaurant telephone.

The caller, who swore at her and called her stupid, had tracked her down through PleaseRobMe.com, a site whose unsubtle name reflected its purpose: to warn people about the risks of geotagging by aggregating and publicizing location data from users of those networks. In Bugbee's case, the warning was effective. She quit foursquare. She started hiring a house sitter. She became, as she put it, a "geotagging curmudgeon."

"I think that a lot of people have drunk the Kool-Aid without actually thinking that hard about it," Bugbee said about location-based technologies. "At some point, some tragedy will occur."

PleaseRobMe shut down last spring after a string of incidents like Bugbee's suggested it may be more helpful to would-be criminals than to users. Nevertheless, its founders said they had accomplished their goal of educating users about the risks of broadcasting their location to the world.

"What is often forgotten is that you're not really talking to a small group of friends," said Douglas Salane, director of the Center for Cybercrime Studies at the John Jay College of Criminal Justice. "You're potentially talking to anyone on the internet."

This can be incredibly useful for law enforcement.

In the world of social networks and applications, location-based services are the next big thing. . . . As more emerge around the digital world, they will leave millions of pieces of location information in their digital wake.

Salane, who has worked with the Manhattan District Attorney and the FBI [Federal Bureau of Investigation], notes that "one of the most useful devices for law enforcement is a cell phone." But at the same time, he adds, users have largely ignored the longer term risks to privacy and public safety.

Our Digital Trail

About 59 percent of American adults now use wireless Internet, up nine percent from one year ago, according to a Pew report on Internet use. About 76 percent use their mobile device to take pictures, and 54 percent have used it to send a photo or video.

And things are getting more complex. The future of the Internet—Web 3.0, if you will—will likely rely heavily on information that users produce and broadcast, either willingly or unwillingly.

In the world of social networks and applications, location-based services are the next big thing. Twitter and Google already use them. Facebook, which hit 500 million users in July, plans to roll out a location-based feature any day now. As more emerge around the digital world, they will leave millions of pieces of location information in their digital wake.

And a small but growing number of programmers are trying to do something about it.

Ben Jackson and Larry Pesce had both safety and privacy in mind when they started ICanStalkU.com in May. With $1,000 and some programming language, the New England-based securities information researchers picked up where PleaseRobMe left off.

ICanStalkU automatically searches thousands of photos on Twitter for geotags, tiny location markers attached to about three percent of all photos posted to the micro blogging site. Then it turns them into a location message, showing how photos can be used to trace people in real time, using information many have no idea they have put out there.

Despite the eyes-in-the-dark logo and dramatic name, Jackson said they intended the site to teach rather than threaten. "We just want people to make an informed decision," explained Jackson. "If they are posting this information, we want them to know what kind of risk this entails."

Stalking in Cyberspace

Stalking experts say the rapid evolution in locational technology has upped the risks. "It doesn't cause stalking but it makes stalking a lot easier," said Rebecca Dreke, a senior analyst at the National Center for Victims of Crime.

About 25 percent of the 3.4 million people who reported being victims of stalkers during 2005–2006 said they had been stalked using some form of cyber technology such as e-mail or instant messaging, according to the most comprehensive evaluation of data to date. The data, reported in a 2009 study by the Department of Justice, predated the wide use of newer technology such as geotagging and may thus seriously underestimate the scope of the problem, says Dreke, who points out that many of those exposed to location-based tracking will not even know they are being watched.

Dreke helps educate law enforcement about how they might use the same technology to help uncover the offenders. It's an uphill battle. "The offenders and the criminals are usually keeping ahead of the people investigating the crime," she said.

A recent study by the security company Webroot showed many social network users are aware of the perils of their digital life. Webroot found 32 percent of men and 49 percent of women reported being "highly concerned" about stalkers. More than half of the 1,500 respondents worried about the privacy implications of their geo-tagged lifestyles.

Todd Zwillich shares their anxiety.

Zwillich, the Washington correspondent for the Public Radio International program, *The Takeaway*, was driving around the capital on a recent Saturday when he spotted a blue Chrysler with the license number NCC1701. He grabbed a friend's iPhone, and ran into traffic to snap a shot of the "awesome" plate. "It's awesome because that is the ID number of the Starship Enterprise," said Zwillich, with a laugh.

Zwillich knew the image would lay bare his Trekkie obsession to friends and followers. But until ICanStalkU picked it up and *The Crime Report* contacted him, Zwillich didn't know he was tagged as standing "nearby 669 New York Avenue NW Washington DC" that day.

Locational data can be culled from information we've opted to offer up to private companies—information emitted by our cell phone and collected by our service provider, pictures we've posted on Twitter, or profile information on Facebook.

The idea didn't sit well. "I'm not interested in having constant GPS [global positioning system] social surveillance," he said. "It's information I want to control."

But increasingly complex privacy settings and out of date laws can make that hard to do. In the courts and on Capitol Hill, debates have begun about how to fashion laws governing cell phone records and electronic communications that strike the right balance between safety and privacy.

Geo-Location and Civil Liberties

Locational data can be culled from information we've opted to offer up to private companies—information emitted by our cell phone and collected by our service provider, pictures we've posted on Twitter, or profile information on Facebook.

The Constitution protects our privacy rights with respect to government prying. Private companies, on the other hand, may collect information on their users and often have wide leeway to use it as they see fit.

Often, that means cooperating with government. Recently, law enforcement has been using the Stored Communications Act to access locational data from cell phone providers, which requires law enforcement agencies to provide "reasonable grounds" before being granted the right to access location records from cell phone companies as well as social media networks like Facebook and Twitter.

The right to do so can help catch criminals and save lives, said Jack Killorin, director of a federal anti-drug task force in Atlanta. Like the FBI and NYPD [New York Police Department], his agency has used location data emitted from cell phones in a number of cases, such as tracking a load of narcotics on the move.

"Where its certainly immediately helpful is when it's used to track down victims of kidnapping, or fugitives," said Killorin, who downplayed privacy concerns about this kind of technology.

"I don't think that there's a threat to the privacy of the overwhelming majority of citizens of the United States," he said. "At least not from law enforcement."

Gray Areas

But law enforcement is already moving into some gray areas that raise questions not just about government access to data, but how it uses the data it collects.

Most people's intuitions about their privacy and public space are wrong or out of date.

Recently, police in a suburb of Dallas, Texas received $60,000 in federal stimulus funds to set up a license plate scanning system, a database of snapshots it can use to keep and track plate numbers to look for stolen cars or kidnap victims. The technology allows the department to track where and when any plate has been photographed, potentially offering up a map of how many of the city's citizens spend their day—where they live, shop, eat, sleep, meet up with lovers and go to political meetings.

The legal scope for using this information is still murky, says Andrew Blumberg, a professor of mathematics at the University of Texas, who has done extensive work on locational privacy.

"Most people's intuitions about their privacy and public space are wrong or out of date," adds Blumberg, which is why he welcomes sites such as PleaseRobMe and ICanStalkU as useful counterforces to the notion that citizens have nothing to fear, as long as the users of such metadata act responsibly.

"Is it legal to keep (such information) forever?" wonders Blumberg, who co-authored a paper on locational privacy with the San Francsico-based Electronic Frontier Foundation, which defends privacy rights in cyberspace. "We need to have a national debate about what the right legislation is."

The debate has started. The law currently governing the use of email communication is the 1986 Electronic Communications Privacy Act. In an unusual show of cooperation, privacy advocates, tech companies and service providers from the ACLU [American Civil Liberties Union] to Facebook have come together to form Digital Due Process, a coalition seeking to update the law for the modern webbed world.

The courts may soon weigh in as well. A case now pending before the Third Circuit Court of Appeals will rule on whether the government should show "probable cause" before obtaining location records from cell phone providers, as it would for a warrant—rather than the present lower standard of "reasonable cause."

In February 2008, a lower-court judge sided with the coalition of digital rights and civil liberties organizations that brought the suit, which included the Electronic Frontier Foundation, the Center for Democracy and Technology and the American Civil Liberties Union. But the Justice Department says the judge was wrong. "An individual has no Fourth Amendment-protected privacy interest in business records," argued DOJ [Department of Justice] lawyer Mark in a brief submitted to Third Circuit defending the current standard.

But ICanStalkU's Ben Jackson isn't sure the law can ever keep up. That's why he and others on the cutting edge of technology will likely keep setting up sites to show the world the digital breadcrumbs they have left behind.

Jackson is already thinking beyond geotagging. The question stuck in his mind is: "What's going to happen next year and the year after that to information I don't know I'm giving out now?"

11

Location-Based Social Networking Can Be Designed to Protect Privacy

Christina Bonnington

Christina Bonnington is a staff writer for Wired *magazine's* Gadget Lab, *covering technology ranging from Apple products to robotics.*

Apps with geolocation features that secretly pull real-time data from other location-based apps and services are creepy and pose security risks. And apps that take content willingly shared on social networks and make it available to strangers elsewhere violate users' sense of privacy. Developers, however, can avoid designing creepy apps by assuring transparency and user control. For apps that constantly transmit data, e-mails and texts can remind users that their data is being monitored. "Ambient notices" that pop up on mobile devices can also alert users when an app shares their location. Finally, users should be able to opt out sharing this information before downloading a location-based app.

Sometimes an app pushes the boundaries of what's socially acceptable—and it fails miserably. Such is the case with the most recent offender, the check-in-based pariah called Girls Around Me.

"In the mood for love, or just a one night stand?" the app's website asks. The query wouldn't be problematic if the app supported an opt-in dating service. But it doesn't. It's an app that was using public information from Foursquare check-ins and Facebook to provide voyeuristic, opportunistic gentlemen the chance to scope out local women.

"Was" is an operative word here. Foursquare pulled its API [application programming interface] access because Girls Around Me was just too creepy (and violated their terms).

And so enters the controversy: All of the location data siphoned down by the app was willingly surrendered by Foursquare users. But the way the app used that data was inherently creepy, and highlighted the potential security risks of broadcasting one's location across social media.

"Context is everything," EFF [Electronic Frontier Foundation] digital rights analyst Rebecca Jeschke told *Wired* via email. "This may not be illegal, but app developers should note the public outcry—the consensus here is that this is, in fact, socially unacceptable and super creepy."

What Makes an App Creepy?

But what is creepy? What precisely makes us feel creeped out about an app?

"I think it's anything that allows somebody who you don't know, or don't interact with, or don't want to interact with, to retrieve more information about you than you're comfortable with," Kevin Mahaffey, CTO [chief technology officer] and cofounder of Lookout Mobile Security told *Wired*. "That's the trigger that borders on creepy in people's minds."

Color was another app that transitioned from cool to ick as users realized nearby strangers would be able to view their photos on the social network—and they could potentially get an eyeful of whatever that person wanted to share, as well.

Nick Doty, a Ph.D. student studying privacy and web standards at UC [University of California] Berkeley's School of Information, pointed out a few themes that arise among "creepy" apps.

"In some cases, it may just be a sense of surprise. The user isn't aware information is being used in a particular way, and when they realize it's being shared or used differently, that can feel like a violation," Doty said. "In other cases, it can be the context. Information is shared in one context and reused in another one that's unexpected or has a different implication."

Developers already have the tools to make sure users are aware of geolocation features in apps, and it's incumbent on them to use them.

Girls Around Me is just one example of that fractured context scenario. Users willingly shared their information within Foursquare or Facebook, but were potentially unaware that this data could be used by third-party party boys.

Over-reaching advertising can also creep us out, Doty says. Say you're using a restaurant search app, and you're aware that it's using your GPS [global positioning system] location to help find businesses near you. You're OK with that. But perhaps the app doesn't also tell you that it's using your location for another purpose: to help advertisers better create a profile of you for targeted advertising.

"That's a pretty common problem—these secondary uses that don't seem related to the app's functionality," Doty said.

Transparency and User Control Are Key

Thus, transparency and user control are key to keeping an app from coming across as untrustworthy or creepy. Developers already have the tools to make sure users are aware of geolocation features in apps, and it's incumbent on them to use them.

For apps that constantly transmit data, like Find My Phone, it would be helpful to regularly send texts or emails notifying the device owner of the continued data monitoring, Doty suggests, as tools like this are sometimes used by abusive ex-partners.

Mobile devices could also employ "ambient notice" features to let users know when location data is being shared. For example, when you're using your iPhone's compass, you can see the phone's arrow symbol and know your device is currently using that feature. Similar signposting could be used for location services.

And, of course, dialog boxes that pop up upon first downloading an app give users a chance to opt-out of location data sharing. These could be augmented to disclose greater detail on what information is collected, and where it might end up. In fact, there are efforts to develop a voluntary code of conduct for location-based apps, according to Mark Uncapher, director of regulatory and government affairs at the Telecommunications Industry Association.

As for Girls Around Me, after Foursquare revoked access to its API, the app developers removed it from the App Store. But the app will be back, apparently. Product lead Vlad Vishnyakov told *Wired* via email that his company will be changing the application name to be gender neutral, and will make the app design "less provocative," among other changes to meet Foursquare's API requirements. [As of August 2013, Girls Around Me is not in the App store.]

"Addressing these concerns is an important part of having a successful business model in the space," Uncapher told *Wired*. "Consumers need to feel comfortable sharing information or they won't share it."

12

Location-Based Social Networking Can Enhance Higher Education

Tim Nekritz

Tim Nekritz is director of web communication and associate director of public affairs at the State University of New York at Oswego.

Colleges and universities can benefit from exploring the use of location-based social networking to engage students in innovative ways, manage their social media presence, and build their communities. Institutions can partner with platforms like Foursquare and Facebook Places to brand themselves and promote their activities and events. Prospective and incoming students can use location-based services in campus tours and to become familiar with university life, earning badges and rewards wherever they check in. Alumni associations can also employ these applications to help attendees reconnect with each other by checking in at reunions. One challenge, however, is that not everyone is eager to use location-based services.

Last October [in 2010], a NASA astronaut checked in from space using Foursquare, a location-based social networking service that allows users to share their location with friends. The next month, the Pew Research Center released a report that said only 4 percent of U.S. adults use these services—and only 1 percent uses them on "any given day." But a statistically significant 8 percent of 18- to 29-year-olds use them—a demographic prized by most marketers.

Savannah Schlaufman, a freshman at Adams State College in Colorado, began using her smart phone to explore her new campus surroundings and connect with friends on Foursquare last July and soon got caught up in the competition to become the "mayor"—one of the virtual badges users receive when they "check in" to a single location more than anyone else—of various spots on campus and around her new college town. While Adams State doesn't have an official Foursquare presence yet, Schlaufman's experience using it is one reason some college administrators have been thinking about whether and how to take the leap into location-based services, which are also known as geosocial networking services.

While users may enjoy the friendly competition that comes with the game-like aspect of these platforms, their potential as marketing tools is likely more appealing to educational institutions.

These platforms, which often incorporate gaming elements like badges and prizes, are downloadable applications that use the GPS [global positioning system] capabilities of users' Internet-enabled mobile devices and smart phones to pinpoint users' locations and enable them to notify their friends of their whereabouts by "checking in." (They can also be used from a mobile website.) Friends may learn of their check-in because they're subscribed to the same location-based service, or they may see it on the feed in their Facebook or Twitter account.

"Location-based services have enormous potential to connect people to places, places to people, and people to people in places," says Tim Jones, director of Web communications at North Carolina State University, which aggregates several geosocial platforms in its community-building activities. "The challenge is in figuring out how best to encourage, support, and develop those connections, and make them relevant and meaningful for your community."

The Next Big Thing or Another Shiny Object?

Location-based services have interesting implications for campus tours and orientations, events promotion, and community building, but deciding which one to use, especially in a burgeoning marketplace, can be confusing. Add to that last August's announcement of Facebook Places—the social networking juggernaut's own location-based service—and institutions may be tempted to watch from the sidelines. The user base of Foursquare and its location-based brethren like Gowalla [which shut down in March 2012], Loopt (which has a suite of mobile applications), and Whrrl may be little more than 10 million users combined—a drop in the bucket compared with Facebook's half-billion users—but many institutions have been experimenting with them in the few years they've been around.

And that's precisely what Ian Hsu, director of Internet media outreach at California's Stanford University, suggests they should be doing. Hsu recommends looking beyond the lure of the trend to explore the platforms and figure out what goals the tools can meet. And while it's worth exploring all the options, matching the desired tasks and audiences involved should determine use, he says.

While users may enjoy the friendly competition that comes with the game-like aspect of these platforms, their potential as marketing tools is likely more appealing to educational institutions. Users can claim prizes, special offers, or discounts for checking in at a certain location. A restaurant or bookstore situated near a popular check-in location may offer incentives to users to drop in. Users can then comment about the deal they just received and push the message out to friends via Facebook or Twitter, thereby extending the reach of the promotion by virtual word of mouth—the essential currency of social media.

That's essentially how David Rosen, a senior at New York's Syracuse University who helps develop and manage the university's social media presence, became affiliated with Foursquare. When he saw that Harvard University in Massachusetts had a branded presence on the service, Rosen tweeted at Dennis Crowley, co-founder of Foursquare and a Syracuse alumnus, that his alma mater should be represented as well. Crowley agreed, and Syracuse joined Stanford and Texas A&M University as the first group of branded institutions on Foursquare. Syracuse uses it to promote events, such as the campus' Orange Central homecoming week. It has held sign-ups, T-shirt giveaways, and other events to promote activities as well as the partnership. Today, Syracuse's Foursquare page boasts more than 4,000 friends.

Gowalla, another geosocial service, lets users post photos and comments about places they've been and create trips as a way to share their favorite places with friends.

Early fall 2010 saw the launch of Foursquare for Universities, an expansion that brought a deluge of requests from institutions, including one from my own, the State University of New York at Oswego. After months of waiting and at least two rounds of paperwork, we received official approval in mid-November. While SUNY Oswego had already developed an independent Foursquare presence, a branded partnership brought with it a certain cachet—along with desirable exclusive campus badges for users to unlock. Badges offer a way to reward check-ins at lectures, athletic games, and artistic events to promote greater campus engagement and awareness of the activities themselves.

Know Your Place

Retailers and restaurants may be attuned to the appeal of the incentives they can offer to this plugged-in crowd of users, but campus marketers are also aware of the benefits that can come from prospective students, young alumni, and other audiences using these services to connect during a campus visit. Part of the appeal of Foursquare lies in the helpful tips and informative reviews that people leave about venues, Rosen says. "When someone is following Syracuse on Foursquare, our tips will be pushed to them when they check in near a venue we have chosen."

Stanford uses Foursquare as a kind of unofficial campus tour that offers "fun, novel, offbeat" information, says Hsu. For example, visitors near the Gates Computer Science Building can stop in to see a piece of Internet history—five disk drives housed in a cabinet made of duct tape and Lego Duplo blocks, aka Google's first server (before it was Google and when its founders were graduate students). "It's more for a sense of history of the place and opportunities for visitors to learn about what's around them," Hsu says.

Gowalla, another geosocial service, lets users post photos and comments about places they've been and create trips as a way to share their favorite places with friends. Subscribers can earn pins and accumulate stamps for their virtual passports when they check in at locations around the world. Several institutions, including SUNY Oswego, the University of Florida, and The University of Oklahoma, have used the trips feature to create official campus tours.

The SUNY Oswego tour, which was developed as a kind of one-man experiment, includes 20 sites ranging from the admissions office to an art gallery. And while it got a lot of hits from being linked to some well-trafficked Web pages, there were very few check-ins. Users may not have been able to properly access the tour if they weren't on campus, or, more likely, those who tried to access the tour were not Gowalla subscribers.

Gowalla is a potentially promising application for alumni associations because it can also be used as a "floating platform," a kind of moving location. Touring bands have used the service to enable a check-in location that follows them from city to city. Alumni associations could use a similar approach for regional reunions where attendees would be able not only to see who is attending an event at their physical location, but also to connect with friends who check in at other reunion sites.

The location-based platform SCVNGR is basically a high-tech scavenger hunt that supports video, photos, and text. From Southern New Hampshire University to Southern Oregon University, more than 350 institutions have integrated the service into their orientation programs to make a game out of familiarizing students with their campuses. SUNY Oswego developed a game in which teams of freshmen had to check into 21 locations to learn about key campus offices, operations, and facts. After performing a prescribed task or learning the correct answer, the team entered the answer into their mobile device to find out the next clue and earn points. Many participants literally ran from place to place in pursuit of bragging rights as well as the hoodie sweatshirts that were awarded to winning teams.

Another multimedia-rich geosocial networking platform, Whrrl, has been involved in the other end of the college experience—graduation. Last May, St. Edward's University in Texas commemorated its 125th anniversary while looking ahead to the future "by conducting the first-ever socially connected graduation," says Mischelle R. Diaz, director of communications. Rather than have students and family members tweeting and posting comments and pictures to their individual Facebook accounts, the university wanted the participants to have a collective experience through Whrrl, which enables multimedia sharing and connects users based on common interests. Since Whrrl was new to most of the university community, St. Edward's began a promotional campaign that included live demonstrations and account sign-up sessions at pregraduation events, posts about it on Facebook and Twitter, e-mails to graduating students, and alerts to campus and local media outlets. In the end, the event captured the observations and eyewitness moments of more than 180 people.

"This allowed graduates and their families to see photos and texts from everyone at the event, not just the photos they were able to take themselves," says Diaz. "We took our cues about the success of the project from the audience reactions during the live slide show—there was lots of laughter and enthusiasm." Afterward, the university posted links to the slide show on its Facebook page, which is also accessible on Whrrl.

When Facebook, the reigning social networking platform, announced Places, many predicted the demise of the other location-based services.

About a month after the St. Edward's graduation experiment, Stanford tried something similar during its 2010 commencement week with the reward-based application Looptstar. Students who downloaded it could follow their friends and unlock a Class of 2010 digital gift as a reward for checking into a certain number of events. The idea behind the project, which was done in conjunction with the Stanford Alumni Association, was to help students connect to the university, to one another during commencement, and as alumni before leaving campus. The project was a moderate success, according to Stanford's Hsu, who added that every foray into geosocial media is a learning experience that provides ideas for future projects.

Are You Game?

Soon after Facebook announced its Places service, the University of Kentucky embraced it and began to promote checking in on campus by marking some of its most-visited locations with large 3-D reproductions of the Facebook Places icon. The campaign is also trying to address privacy, the main concern these location-based services present, on a prominent section of its website (*www.uky.edu/facebook*) by showing users how to customize their settings and explaining the effects of selecting certain privacy settings. Window clings and posters with the website address cover campus. These simulated Facebook Places icons—in Kentucky blue—identify campus locations, attractions, and events.

When Facebook, the reigning social networking platform, announced Places, many predicted the demise of the other location-based services. Instead, Foursquare had a record number of signups within 24 hours due to the attention Facebook received. That may be part of the role Facebook plays in this particular game.

"As Facebook got users to be more comfortable with sharing their personal lives, and more comfortable using Twitter, Facebook Places [may help] make users more comfortable with sharing their location," says Rosen of Syracuse, adding that it may also act as a gateway geosocial service for other, richer platforms. But therein lies the stickiest point of these platforms: Some people may never be comfortable sharing their location.

Organizations to Contact

The editors have compiled the following list of organizations concerned with the issues debated in this book. The descriptions are derived from materials provided by the organizations. All have publications or information available for interested readers. The list was compiled on the date of publication of the present volume; names, addresses, phone and fax numbers, and e-mail and Internet addresses may change. Be aware that many organizations take several weeks or longer to respond to inquiries, so allow as much time as possible.

American Civil Liberties Union (ACLU)
125 Broad St., 18th Floor, New York, NY   10004
(212) 549-2500
e-mail: aclu@aclu.org
website: www.aclu.org

The American Civil Liberties Union (ACLU) is a national organization that works to defend civil rights as guaranteed in the Constitution. It publishes various materials, papers, and blogs on civil liberties, including the national newsletter *Civil Liberties* and a set of handbooks on individual rights. "If It's Reasonable in Denver: Lessons in Location Tracking from Colorado" and "Your Cell Phone Knows Where You Were Last Night . . . Who Else Does?" are two of its blog articles on cell phones and location-based data.

Center for Democracy and Technology (CDT)
1634 I St. NW, Suite 1100, Washington, DC   20006
(202) 637-9800 • fax: (202) 637-0968
website: www.cdt.org

The mission of the Center for Democracy and Technology (CDT) is to develop public policy solutions that advance constitutional civil liberties and democratic values in new computer and communications media. Pursuing its mission through policy research, public education, and coalition building, the Center works to increase citizens' privacy and the public's control over the use of personal information held by government and other institutions. Its publications include issue briefs, policy papers, and CDT Policy Posts.

CTIA—The Wireless Association

1400 16th St. NW, Suite 600, Washington, DC   20036
(202) 736-3200 • fax: (202) 785-0721
website: www.ctia.org

CTIA is an international nonprofit membership organization that has represented the wireless communications industry since 1984. The association advocates on behalf of its members at all levels of government. CTIA also coordinates the industry's voluntary efforts to provide consumers with a variety of choices and information regarding their wireless products and services. This includes the voluntary industry guidelines, including "Best Practices and Guidelines for Location-Based Services." Online, the association offers a blog, e-mail news briefings, and multimedia library.

Electronic Frontier Foundation (EFF)

815 Eddy St., San Francisco, CA   94109
(415) 436-9333 • fax: (415) 436-9993
e-mail: info@eff.org
website: www.eff.org

The Electronic Frontier Foundation (EFF) is an organization of students and other individuals that aims to promote a better understanding of telecommunications issues. It fosters awareness of civil liberty issues arising from advancements in computer-based communications media and supports litigation to preserve, protect, and extend First Amendment rights in computing and telecommunications technologies. EFF's publications include the electronic newsletter *EFFector Online*, online bulletins, and publications, including the annual report *Who's Got Your Back?*

Electronic Privacy Information Center (EPIC)

1718 Connecticut Ave. NW, Suite 200, Washington, DC   20009
(202) 483-1140 • fax: (202) 483-1248
website: www.epic.org

As an advocate of the public's right to electronic privacy, the Electronic Privacy Information Center (EPIC) sponsors educational and research programs, compiles statistics, and conducts litigation pertaining to privacy and other civil liberties. Its publications include the biweekly electronic newsletter *EPIC Alert* and news and information on locational and consumer privacy.

Federal Trade Commission (FTC)

600 Pennsylvania Ave. NW, Washington, DC   20580
(202) 326-2222
website: www.ftc.gov

The Federal Trade Commission (FTC) deals with issues that touch the economic life of every American. It is the only federal agency with both consumer protection and competition jurisdiction in broad sectors of the economy. Its website offers information on mobile telecommunications, handheld devices, and smartphone applications, including issues relating to consumer privacy.

Mobile Marketing Association (MMA)

PO Box 3963, Bellevue, WA   98009-3963
(646) 257-4515
e-mail: mma@mmaglobal.com
website: www.mmaglobal.com

The Mobile Marketing Association (MMA) is a nonprofit trade association representing all players in the mobile marketing value chain. It works to promote, educate, measure, guide, and protect the mobile marketing industry worldwide. One of the organization's objectives is to define and publish mobile marketing best practices and guidelines on privacy, ad delivery, and ad measurement. MMA publishes a newsletter and the *International Journal of Mobile Marketing*.

Privacy Rights Clearinghouse (PRC)
3108 Fifth Ave., Suite A, San Diego, CA   92103
(619) 298-3396
website: www.privacyrights.org

Privacy Rights Clearinghouse (PRC) is a nonprofit consumer organization with a two-part mission—to provide consumer information and advocate for consumer privacy. The group raises awareness of how technology affects personal privacy, empowers consumers to take action to control their own personal information by providing practical tips on privacy protection, responds to privacy-related complaints from consumers, and reports this information. Its website provides transcripts of PRC speeches and testimony, stories of consumer experiences, and numerous fact sheets, including "Wireless Communications: Voice and Data Privacy" and "Privacy in the Age of the Smartphone."

Bibliography

Books

Ben Agger — *Oversharing: Presentations of Self in the Internet Age.* New York: Routledge, 2011.

Richard F. Ferraro and Murat Aktihanoglu — *Location-Aware Applications.* Shelter Island, NY: Manning Publications, 2011.

Jennifer Golbeck — *Analyzing the Social Web.* Waltham, MA: Morgan Kaufmann, 2013.

Ed Gordon and Adriana de Souza e Silva — *Net Locality: Why Location Matters in a Networked World.* Malden, MA: Wiley-Blackwell, 2011.

Jeff Jarvis — *Public Parts: How Sharing in the Digital Age Improves the Way We Work and Live.* New York: Simon & Schuster, 2011.

Rich Ling and Scott W. Campell — *Mobile Communication: Bringing Us Together and Tearing Us Apart.* New Brunswick, NJ: Transaction Publishers, 2011.

Chuck Martin — *The Third Screen: Marketing to Your Customers in a World Gone Mobile.* Boston: Nicholas Brealey, 2011.

Daniel Rowles — *Mobile Marketing: How Mobile Technology Is Revolutionizing Marketing, Communications, and Advertising.* London: Kogan Page, 2013.

Michael Saylor	*The Mobile Wave: How Mobile Intelligence Will Change Everything.* New York: Vanguard Press, 2012.
Adriana de Souza e Silva and Jordan Frith	*Mobile Interfaces in Public Spaces: Locational Privacy, Control, and Urban Sociability.* New York: Routledge, 2012.
Anthony M. Townsend	*Smart Cities: Big Data, Civic Hackers, and the Quest for a New Utopia.* New York: W.W. Norton, 2013.

Periodicals and Internet Sources

Tim Beyers and Karl Thiel	"Will Location-Based Social Networks Be the Next Facebook?," The Motley Fool, March 15, 2012. www.fool.com.
Joshua Brustein	"Do Consumers Want Location-Based Social Networking?," *New York Times*, November 6, 2010.
The Economist	"Location-Based Social Networks: Where Are You?," August 26, 2010.
Preston Gralla, Al Sacco, and Ryan Faas	"Smartphone Apps: Is Your Privacy Protected?," *Computerworld*, July 7, 2011.
Andrew Hough	"Please Rob Me Website Causes Fury for 'Telling Burglars When Twitter Users Are Not Home,'" *Telegraph*, February 19, 2010.
Eric Lichtblau	"Police Are Using Phone Tracking as a Routine Tool," *New York Times*, March 31, 2012.

Jim Louderback	"How Location-Based Social Networking Gets Creepy," *Advertising Age*, May 12, 2010.
Dana Mattioli and Miguel Bustillo	"Can Texting Save Stores?," *Wall Street Journal*, May 8, 2012.
Brian Proffitt	"Location-Based Services: Are They There Yet?," *Computerworld*, May 3, 2012.
Matthew J. Schwartz	"Smartphone Invader Tracks Your Every Move," *InformationWeek*, November 15, 2011.
Lauren Silverman	"Smartphone Apps Help More Singles Find the Boy (Or Girl) Next Door," All Tech Considered, August 20, 2012. www.npr.org/blogs /alltechconsidered.
R "Ray" Wang	"Why I'm Unplugging from Location Based Services Until the Privacy Issue Is Resolved," Enterprise Irregulars, January 17, 2011. www.enterprise irregulars.com.

Index